WEEDS USED IN MEDICINE

FARMERS BULLETIN 188

I0456209

First Edition 1917
Alice Henkel

New Edition 2017

Edited by Tarl Warwick
Illustrated by Rita Metzner

COPYRIGHT AND DISCLAIMER

FOREWORD

In the early days of the 20th century it was common for businesses, banks, government firms, and other groups to release short circulations on monographic topics related to the function of agriculture and industry. This is one of those titles from the same era, roughly a century ago- in particular, on the topic of some pestilent and (slightly arbitrarily) classified "weeds" which at the time farmers were legally required to attempt to exterminate on their property. Apparently concerned that this would prove burdensome, the government determined that it would counter the cost in terms of manpower and time to remove said species by informing the agricultural community that some species were able, properly preserved, to be sold as a medicinal commodity.

Some of the species listed here are poisonous- few are used anymore outside of the realm of alternative medicine, however, this little herbal of sorts is still useful for identification and as a historical piece on the medicine of the early 1900s. A few of the species in this guide are still sold today for purposes unrelated to medicine; such as catnip, which is of course commonly sold as an entertaining product for those of a feline disposition.

This edition of "Weeds as Medicine" has been re-illustrated, as well as edited for grammar and format. Care has been taken to retain all original intent and meaning.

WEEDS USED IN MEDICINE

INTRODUCTION

It is a matter of interest, primarily to the farmer, that certain of the well-known weeds now either generally or locally infesting the country are the sources of crude drugs at the present time obtained wholly or in part by importation from abroad. Roots, leaves, and flowers of several of the species most detrimental in the United States are gathered, prepared, and cured in Europe, and not only form useful commodities there but supply to a considerable extent the demands of foreign lands. Hence it appears probable that while weeds can hardly be made desirable, still in his fight to exterminate them the farmer may be able to turn some of them to account. Some of the plants coming within this class are in many States at present subject to antiweed laws and farmers are required to take measures toward their extermination. It seems, therefore, desirable to make these pests sources of profit where possible. In many cases, when weeds have been dug, the work of handling and curing them is not excessive and can readily be done by women and children.

The prices paid for crude drugs from these sources are not great and would rarely tempt anyone to pursue this line of work as a business. Yet, if in ridding the farm of weeds and thus raising the value of the land the farmer can at the same time make these pests the source of a small income instead of a dead loss, something is gained. In order to help the farmer to obtain the best possible prices for such products, instructions for collecting and preparing crude drugs derived from weeds are here briefly given. The collector should observe them carefully.

WEEDS USED IN MEDICINE

COLLECTION AND CURING OF DRUGS

Too much emphasis can not be placed upon the importance of carefully and thoroughly drying all crude drugs, whether roots, herbs, leaves, barks, flowers, or seeds. If insufficiently dried, they will heat and become moldy in shipping, and the collector will find his goods rejected by the drug dealer and have all his trouble for nothing.

Another important matter to be considered in collecting drugs for market is freedom from foreign substances. All drugs should be clean and wholesome looking and contain no admixture of fragments of other plants, stones, dirt, or other impurities. A bright natural color is extremely desirable in leaves, herbs, and flowers, and adds much to the worth of the product. This can be readily brought about by giving careful attention to proper drying in the shade (not in direct sunlight), and by protection from dew or rain by placing the drugs under cover at nightfall or whenever necessary. Roots may be cleaned by washing, but leaves, herbs, and flowers should never be washed.

It is important also to collect drugs in proper season only. Neglect in this respect will bring nothing but disappointment to the gatherer, as drugs collected out of season not only are not acceptable to the dealer on account of inferior medicinal qualities, but there will also be, in the case of roots, a greater amount of shrinkage in a root dug during the growing season than will take place when it is collected after growth has ceased.

The collector should be sure that the plant he is collecting is the right one. There are many plants that closely resemble one another, yet one may possess medicinal properties and the other be absolutely useless. Again, a plant may contain very poisonous principles, and if represented to be something else, it might of course do untold injury.

It would therefore be best, where any doubt exists, to send a specimen of the entire plant, including leaves, flowers, and fruits, to a drug dealer or to the nearest State experiment station for identification.

ROOTS

Roots should never be collected during the growing season, as at that time they are deficient in medicinal properties, and they also shrink more in drying and weigh less than when gathered at full maturity. The roots of annual plants should be dug just before the flowering period, and those of biennial or perennial plants after the tops have dried, the former in the autumn of the first year and the latter in the fall of the second or third year.

After the roots have been dug1 the adherent soil should be well shaken from them, and all foreign particles, such as stones, dirt, roots and parts of other plants, should be removed. If the roots can not be sufficiently cleared of soil by shaking, they should be thoroughly washed in clean water. It does not pay to be careless in this matter.

The presence of soil increases the weight of the root, but the intending purchaser is not willing to pay for the weight of the dirt, and grades the uncleaned drug accordingly. It is the clean, bright-looking root that will bring a good price.

After washing, the roots should be carefully dried. This can best be accomplished by exposing them to light and air (not direct sunlight) on racks or shelves, or on clean, well-ventilated barn floor, or lofts.

They should be spread out thinly and turned occasionally from day to day until completely cured. When this point is reached, in perhaps three to six weeks, the roots will snap readily when bent. During the curing process the roots, if dried out of doors, should be placed under shelter at night and upon the approach of rainy weather. With some roots additional preparation is required, such as slicing and the removal of fibrous rootlets. Wherever this is necessary mention will be made of it under the descriptions of the different plants.

In general, it may be said that large roots should always be split or sliced when green in order to facilitate drying.

BARKS

The plants considered in this bulletin do not furnish medicinal barks, but inasmuch as there are certain sections of the country where trees furnishing such barks are rather abundant, directions for their collection may not be out of place here. Barks of trees should be gathered in spring, when the sap begins to flow, but may also be peeled in winter. In the case of the coarser barks (as elm, hemlock, poplar, oak, pine, and wild cherry) the outer layer is shaved off before the bark is removed from the tree, which process is known as "rossing." Only the inner bark of these trees is used medicinally. Barks may also be cured by exposure to sunlight.

Moisture must be avoided.

LEAVES AND HERBS

Leaves and herbs should be collected when the plants are in full flower. It is very desirable that they retain their bright green color after curing, and this can be done by careful drying in the shade. In the collection of leaves the whole plant may be cut and the leaves may be stripped from it, rejecting the stems M much as possible. In the case of herbs the coarse and large stems should be rejected and only the flowering tops and more tender stems and leaves included.

All grasses, bits of other plants, and other foreign substances should be carefully removed, as well as dead, shriveled, diseased, and discolored specimens.

Both leaves and herbs should be spread out in thin layers on clean floors, racks or shelves, in the shade but where there is free circulation of air, and turned frequently until thoroughly dry. Moisture will darken them. The same precautions that are necessary in curing roots apply here also, so far as placing them under cover to avoid dew or rain is concerned.

FLOWERS

Flowers are collected when they first open or immediately after not when they are beginning to fade. To preserve the bright natural color as nearly as possible they should be carefully dried in the shade, in the same manner as directed for leaves and herbs.

SEEDS

Seeds should be gathered just as "they are ripening, before the seed pods open, and should be winnowed in order to remove fragments of stems, leaves, and shriveled specimens.

DISPOSAL OF THE DRUGS

Samples representative of the lot of drugs to be sold

should be sent to the nearest commission merchant, general store, or drug store, for inspection and for quotation on the amount of drug that can be furnished, or for information as to where to send the article. The size of the sample depends, of course, upon the kind of drug; from 3 to 4 ounces- or, say, at least a good handful- should be submitted. The package containing the sample should be plainly marked as regards contents, and the name and address of the sender given. In writing to the different dealers for information and prices, it should be stated how large a quantity of a particular drug can be furnished and how soon this can be supplied, and postage should always be enclosed for reply. In no case should the entire lot of collected drugs be sent to dealers without preliminary correspondence. The collector should bear in mind that freight is an important item, and it is best, therefore, to address such dealers as are nearest to the place of production.

When ready for shipment, crude drugs may be tightly packed in burlap or gunny sacks, or In dry, clean barrels.

DESCRIPTIONS OF PLANTS

The plants included in this bulletin are burdock, dandelion, the docks, couch grass, and pokeweed (principally root drugs); foxglove, mullein, lobelia, tansy, gum plant, scaly grindelia, boneset, catnip, hoarhound, yarrow, fleabane, blessed thistle, jimson weed, and poison hemlock (of which either the leaves, flowers, herb, or seeds are used in medicine); and also wormseed, and black and white mustards, of which the seeds only are used.

Descriptions of these plants follow, together with the common names by which they are known in different localities, the habitat (or, in other words, the kinds of places or soils in which they are likely to be found), their geographical range, information as to the parts to be collected, their uses, the extent to which they are imported and the prices usually paid by dealers.

The principal uses for which these plants are employed in medicine are briefly indicated, but none of the drugs mentioned should be taken without the advice of a physician.

With the exception of the figures for dandelion and mustard, which were obtained from the Bureau of Statistics of the Department of Commerce and Labor, the imports are based on estimates furnished by dealers, and the prices per pound, while serving to give an idea as to what may be expected for the drugs, will vary from year to year, depending principally upon supply and demand. There are of course a large number of plants used in medicine that are not included in this bulletin, which is intended to cover only such medicinal plants as may be classed as weeds.

BURDOCK
Arcticum lappa L.

Other common names: Cockle button, cuckold dock, beggars' buttons, hurr-bur, stick button, hardock, and bardane.

Habitat and range: Burdock is one of the most common weeds. It was introduced from the Old World, and is common and often very abundant in the Eastern and Central States and in some scattered localities in the West, growing along roadsides, in fields, pastures, and waste places.

Description: This is a coarse, unsightly biennial weed of the aster family (Asteracese), which produces during the first year of its growth only a rosette of large, thin leaves and a long, tapering root having a diameter of from one-half to 1 inch. When full grown it measures from 3 to 7 feet high. The round, fleshy stem is branched, grooved, and hairy, with very large leaves, even in the early stages of the growth of the plant, the lower leaves often measuring 18 inches in length. The leaves are alternate, on long, solid, deeply furrowed leafstalks; thin, roundish or oval, but usually heart shaped; with even, wavy, or toothed margins; smooth above, and pale and woolly on the under surface. The flowers are purple, in the frost. These flower heads are armed with hooked tips, and the burs thus formed are a great pest, attaching themselves to clothing and to the wool and hair of animals. The seed of burdock is produced in great abundance, one plant bearing as many as 400,000 seeds.

Parts used: The root alone is recognized in the United States Pharmacopoeia, but there is a limited demand for burdock seed, and the leaves also are employed. Burdock roots and seeds are used in blood and skin diseases, and the leaves externally as a cooling poultice for swellings and ulcers, the latter being employed only in the fresh state.

Burdock has a large taproot, about 12 inches long, fleshy, the outside blackish-brown or grayish-brown, the inside light in color and spongy in the center. It is to be collected in the fall of the first year. The roots must be washed, split lengthwise, and carefully dried. Drying causes the root to lose about four-fifths of its weight, and to become scaly, and wrinkled lengthwise. Sometimes the bases of the leafstalks remain at the top of the root in the form of a small, white, silky tuft.

The odor of the root is weak and unpleasant. The seeds are oblong, curved, flattened, and angular, dark brown and sometimes spotted with black, and have no odor. These should be collected when ripe or nearly so.

Imports and prices: About 50,000 pounds of lappa or burdock root are imported annually, and the best root is said to come from Belgium, where great care is exercised in its collection. The price of the root ranges from 3 to 8 cents per pound, and that of the seed from 5 to 10 cents.

DANDELION
Taraxacum taraxacum (Karst) *Taraxacum officinale* (Weber)

Other common names: Blow-ball, caankerwort, doon head clock, fortune teller, horse gowan, Irish daisy, yellow gowan, one o'clock.

Range and habitat: Dandelion is distributed as a weed in all civilized parts of the world, and in this country is naturalized from Europe- With the exception of the South, it is very abundant throughout the United States in fields and waste places, and it is especially troublesome in lawns and meadows.

WEEDS USED IN MEDICINE

Description: The dandelion is so well known a weed, especially in lawns, that it scarcely requires a description, almost everyone being familiar with its rosette of coarsely toothed leaves, golden-yellow flowers, and round fluffy seed heads. It is a perennial plant of the chicory family (Cichoriaceae), and it may be said to be in flower throughout almost the entire year. In spring the young leaves are collected and used for greens or salad, but the part employed in medicine is the root. The flowering stem of the dandelion is usually longer than the smooth, shining green, coarsely toothed leaves, reaching a height of from 5 to 10 inches. It is erect, smooth, naked, and hollow, bearing at the summit a solitary yellow flower head, which opens in the morning and only in fair weather. The entire plant contains a white, milky juice.

Part used: As already stated, the root of dandelion is used medicinally. It is a large taproot, sometimes 20 inches long, thick and fleshy, dull-yellow or brownish on the outside, white inside, practically without odor, and bitter. Dandelion is often used as a tonic in diseases of the liver and in dyspepsia.

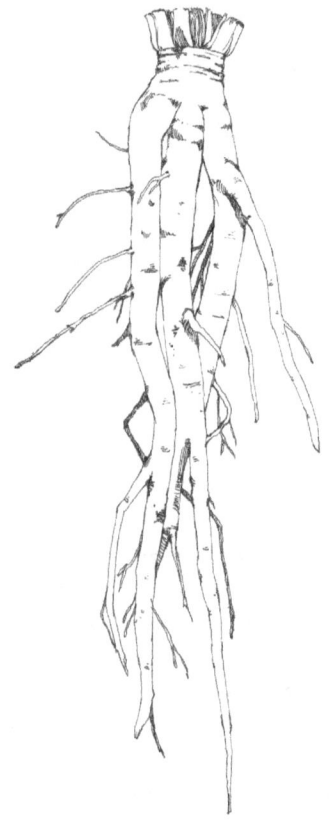

The best time for digging dandelion root Is from July to September, during which time the milky juice becomes thicker and the bitterness increases. It should be carefully washed and thoroughly dried. Dandelion roots decrease considerably in size by drying, weighing less than half as much as the fresh roots and becoming wrinkled lengthwise. The dried root should not be kept too long, as drying diminishes its medicinal virtues.

Imports and prices: During the fiscal year ended June 30, 1903, the imports of taraxacum or dandelion root into the United States amounted to 115,522 pounds. The price per pound ranges from 1 to 6 cents.

DOCKS
Rumex species

Several species of docks possess medicinal properties. Among these are the yellow dock (*Rumex crispus* L.), the broad-leaved dock (*R. obtusifolius* L.) and the yellow-rooted water dock (*R. Britannica* L.) all more or less abundant throughout the United States. Other species are also recognized as possessing value in medicine, but those above mentioned are the kinds generally collected.

Yellow Dock
Rumex crispus L.

Other common names: Curled dock, narrow dock, sour dock.

Range and habitat: The species most commonly employed in medicine is the yellow dock, a perennial introduced from Europe and now found throughout the United States as a troublesome and very persistent weed in cultivated as well as waste ground, among rubbish heaps, and along roadsides.

Description: The deep, spindle-shaped root sends up an erect, angular, and furrowed stem about 2 to 4 feet high, leafy, branching near the top, and bearing numerous elongated clusters of inconspicuous flowers. The leaves are lance shaped, acute, with the margins strongly waved and crisped. The lower leaves are obtuse or heart shaped at the base, from 6 to 8 inches in length, and are borne on long stalks, while those nearer the top are narrower and shorter, being only 3 to 6 inches long, on short stems or stemless.

From June to August the yellow dock puts forth, interspersed with leaves, its many long dense clusters of green, drooping groups of inconspicuous flowers placed in circles around the stem.

Broad-leaved Dock
(Rumex obtusifolius L.)

Other common names: Bitter dock, common dock, blunt-leaved dock, butter dock.

WEEDS USED IN MEDICINE

Range and Habitat: The range of this very common weed extends from the New England States to Oregon and south to Florida and Texas. It occurs in waste places.

Description: Broad Leafed dock differs from the yellow dock principally in its more robust habit of growth. It grows to about the same height, but its stem is stouter, and the leaves, which are wavy along the margin as in the yellow dock, are much broader and longer. The lower loaves have long stalks, and are from 6 to 14 inches in length, with heart-shaped or roundish bases, while the upper ones are from 2 to 6 inches long and are on short stalks. The green flowers appear from June to August, and are in rather groups In all of the docks here mentioned, the three inner divisions of the calyx (outer covering of flower) in fruiting form a kind of triangular nut, like the grain of buckwheat (to which family, Polygonaceae, the docks belong) and one or more of these divisions bear on the back a small granule.

The difference between flower and fruit is barely distinguishable when seen from a little distance so long as the fruit is immature, both being green, but later in the season, as the fruit ripens, the spikes take on a rusty brown color.

Yellow-rooted Water Dock
(Rumex britannica L.)

Habitat and range: As the common name indicates, this plant frequents swampy and wet places and banks of streams. It is found from Canada to New Jersey and Pennsylvania, and westward to Minnesota, Illinois, and Iowa.

Description: The yellow-rooted water dock is a taller plant than either of the docks previously mentioned, its stout stem sometimes reaching a height of 6 feet. The leaves at the base of the plant are borne on long stalks, and are from 1 to 2 feet in length, but, as with the other two species, the leaves toward the top of the plant are shorter, as are also the stalks supporting them. The densely flowered clusters are not as leafy as in the preceding species mentioned. The plant flowers from July to August.

Dock Roots

The root, which is the part to be collected for medicinal purposes, is very similar in all of these species of dock, usually from 8 to 12 inches long, fleshy, often somewhat branched, the outside dark reddish-brown with a rather thick bark, internally yellowish. It possesses but a very faint odor and a bitter, astringent taste. The roots should be collected in late summer or autumn after the fruiting tops have ripened, then washed, split lengthwise into halves or quarters, and carefully dried.

WEEDS USED IN MEDICINE

The docks are largely employed for purifying the blood and as a remedy in skin diseases.

Imports and prices: Rumex or dock roots are imported into this county to the extent of about 125,000 pounds annually. The price ranges from 2 to 8 cents per pound.

WEEDS USED IN MEDICINE

COUCH GRASS

Agropyron repens (L.) Beauv. (Triticum repens L.)

Other common names: Dog-grass, quick-grass, quack-grass, quitchgrass scutch-grass, twitch-grass, witch-grass, wheat-grass, Chandler's grass, creeping wheat-grass, devil's-grass, durfa-grass, Durfee-grass, Dutch-grass, Fin's grass, quake-grass.

Range and habitat: Couch grass, like so many other pernicious weeds, was introduced into this country from Europe, and is now a most troublesome pest in cultivated ground, causing the farmer a loss of thousands of dollars annually by taking possession of fields and crowding out valuable crops. It is most abundant from Maine to Maryland, and westward to Minnesota and Missouri, but is rather sparingly distributed in the South. It is gaining ground on farms on the Pacific slope.

Description: This rather coarse grass produces several stems, 1 to 3 feet high, from a long, creeping, jointed rootstock, and bears densely flowered spike-like heads resembling those of rye or beardless wheat. The stems are round, smooth, thickened at the joints, and hollow, bearing from five to seven leaves. These have a long cleft sheath, and are rough on the upper surface. The heads or spikes are terminal, solitary, compressed, with two rows of spikelets on a wavy and flattened axis.

Couch grass is one of difficult weeds to eradicate, on account of the long jointed rootstock, each joint of which is capable of producing a new plant. Every bit of the rootstock must therefore be removed from the soil or killed in order to eradicate it.

WEEDS USED IN MEDICINE

Part used: The most important part of this grass, not only agriculturally but also pharmaceutically is its long, tough rhizome or rootstock, creeping along underneath the ground and pushing in every direction. It is pale yellow, smooth, about one-eighth of an inch in diameter, with joints at intervals of about an inch from which slender branching rootlets are produced. One of the best methods of destroying this weed is to plow up the roots and burn them. They need not be burned, however, but may be saved and prepared for the drug market. After the rootstocks have been collected and washed the rootlets should be removed and the rhizome or rootstock (not the rootlets) cut into short pieces about two-fifths of an inch long. An ordinary feed-cutting machine may be used for this purpose. These should then be dried as suggested in the general instructions

In the drug trade this plant is generally known as dog

grass or triticum. As found in the stores it is in the form of small, angular pieces, about one eighth to one fourth of an inch long, straw colored, shining, and hollow. These pieces are odorless but have a somewhat sweetish taste.

The fluid extract prepared from dog grass is used in kidney and bladder troubles.

Imports and prices: Couch grass is almost wholly an imported article, some 250,000 pounds coming into this country annually from Europe. The price is about 3 to 7 cents per pound.

POKEWEED

Phytolacca americana L. (Phytolacca decandra L.)

Other common names: Poke, pigeon-berrv, garget, skoke, pocan, coakum, Virginian poke, ink-berry, red ink-berry, American nightshade, cancer jalap, redweed.

Range and habitat: Pokeweed is common in rich, moist soil along fence rows, margins of fields, and in uncultivated land from the New England States to Minnesota and south to Florida and Texas. It is native in this country and naturalized in Europe, where it is regarded as an ornamental garden plant.

Description: The reddish purple stems, rich green foliage, and clusters of white flowers and dark-purple berries give to this plant a rather handsome appearance. Pokeweed attains a height of from 3 to 9 feet from a very large perennial root. It is erect, branched, the stems stout, smooth, green at first, then reddish. On examining a piece of the stem, the pith will be seen to be divided into disk-shaped pieces, with hollow spaces between them. The leaves are ovate or ovate-oblong, acute at the apex, smooth, about 5 inches long and 2 to 3 inches wide, on short stems. The margins are without indentation. About July to September the long clusters of whitish flowers are produced, followed by the green berries, which upon ripening become a rich dark purple color. The flower clusters are from 3 to 4 inches in length and on long stalks, the flowers numerous and borne on reddish stems. The berries are globular, flattened both at top and bottom, smooth and shining, and contain ten black seeds embedded in a rich crimson juice.

Parts used: For medicinal purposes the berries and roots are employed. Both of these should be collected when the berries are fully mature, which usually occurs about two months after flowering. The clusters of berries should be carefully dried in the shade. They are poisonous, have no odor, a sweetish taste at first, then acrid.

Pokeweed has a very large, fleshy, and poisonous root, conical in shape and branched. (Fig. 12.) It should be gathered in the latter part of the fall, thoroughly cleaned, cut into transverse slices, and carefully dried. When dry it has a grayish, wrinkled appearance, breaks with a fibrous fracture, and the slices show many concentric rings. There is a slight odor and the taste is sweetish and acrid.

Both the berries and roots are alterative, act upon the bowels and cause vomiting, and preparations made from them are used in treating various diseases of the skin and blood, and in certain cases in relieving pain and allaying inflammation.

Price: Phytolacca or pokeroot brings from 2 to 5 cents per pound, and the dry berries about 5 cents per pound.

FOXGLOVE
(Digitalis purpurea L.)

Other common names: Purple foxglove, thimbles, fairy cap, fairy fingers, fairy thimbles, fairy bells, dog's finger, finger flower, lady's glove, ladyfingers, lady's thimble, popdock, flapdock, flopdook, lion's mouth, rabbit's flower, cottagers, throatwort, Scotch mercury.

Range and habitat: Foxglove was originally introduced into this country from Europe as an ornamental garden plant, but has now escaped from cultivation in a few localities and is assuming the character of a weed. This is the cast in parts of Oregon, Washington, and West Virginia, where the plant is found in great abundance in dry, sandy soil, along roads and fence rows, on the borders of timber land, and in small cleared places.

Description: This is a very handsome plant of the figwort family (Scrophulariaceae), biennial, and the first year forms only a rosette of dense leaves, but in the second year of its growth the simple erect flowering stalk is produced, attaining a height of from 3 to 4 feet. This is round, indistinctly angled toward the top, leafy and downy. The leaves are oblong-ovate, narrowed at the base into long- winded stalks; the upper surface of the leaves is dull green and wrinkled, while the under side is grayish, with short, soft hairs and a thick network of prominent veins. The root leaves are rather large and are borne on long stalks, but as the leaves approach the top of the plant they become smaller and the leafstalks shorter.

The plant is in flower about June, and the long clusters of numerous tubular bell-shaped flowers are very showy. The clusters are terminal, and about 14 inches in length. The flowers are large, about 2 inches long, the color ranging from white through lavender to purple, the inside of the lower lobe bearing long, soft, white hairs and crimson spots on a white ground.

Part used: Leaves of the second year's growth only are employed, and these should be collected when about two-thirds of the flowers have expanded. They should be very carefully dried in the shade and then kept in close boxes or barrels so as to keep out all moisture. The greatest care is necessary in curing, as the leaves soon lose their medicinal properties if not properly dried.

Preparations made from foxglove are of great value in heart troubles, but they are poisonous and should never be used except on the advice of a physician.

Imports and prices: From 40,000 to 60,000 pounds of digitalis or foxglove are annually imported into this country from Europe, where the plant is cultivated. The American-grown product has so far never been used, but leaves from the wild American plant have been assayed and found to be equally as good as the European article. The price per pound ranges from about 6 to 8 cents.

MULLEIN
Verbascum thapsus L.

Other common names: Great mullein, velvet or mullein dock, Aaron's rod, Adam's flannel, blanket leaf, bullock's lungwort, cow's or clown's lungwort, candlewick, feltwort, flannel leaf, old-man's flannel, hare's beard, hedge taper, ice leaf, Jacob's staff, Jupiter's staff, lady's foxglove, Peter's staff, shepherd's club, torches, torchwort, velvet plant.

Range and Habitat: Mullein is a native of Europe and occurs in this country as a troublesome weed in fields and pastures, waste places, and along roadsides from Maine to Minnesota and southward, and it is also spreading in the far Western States. It produces great quantities of seed, and, if allowed to persist, will sow seeds which may retain their vitality and germinate at intervals for a number of years.

WEEDS USED IN MEDICINE

Description: Mullein can be easily recognized by its tall, erect habit of growth, the white, woolly or felty appearance of the entire plant, and its spike of golden-yellow flowers. It is a biennial belonging to the figwort family (Scrophulariacea).

This plant has a stout, straight stem, which sometimes grows as tall as 7 feet. The stem and also the leaves are densely hairy, the latter mate, sessile (stemless), their margins extending in wings along down the stem. The rather thick, rough leaves are from 4 to 12 inches in length, oblong, acute, and densely hairy above and below. In the first year of its growth only a rosette of downy leaves is produced, but during the second year the flower stalk with its densely flowered spike appears.

The golden-yellow flowers are produced from June to August.

Parts used: As the leaves and flowers are to be collected at the time when the plant is in bloom, the propagation of the plant by the dissemination of its seed is prevented. The leaves are cured in the usual manner. They are practically inodorous, and have a somewhat bitter, mucilaginous taste. It is very desirable to have the flowers retain their bright yellow color; they must therefore be thoroughly dried, and then kept free from moisture in well-stopped bottles. They readily absorb moisture and if allowed to become damp will turn black. The corolla (petals), with the adhering stamens only, is dried, the calyx being rejected. Mullein flowers have a sweetish, pleasant odor.

Mullein is used in coughs and catarrh, to quiet nervous irritation, and to relieve pain and inflammation. According to some authors the dried leaves are often smoked like tobacco to relieve nasal catarrh and throat affections.

Imports and prices: About 5,000 pounds of verbascum or

mullein flowers are annually imported, chiefly from Germany, in which country this plant is cultivated. The leaves are also imported to a small extent. The price paid for the leaves ranges from 2.5 to 5 cents per pound, and that for the flowers may range from 25 to 75 cents per pound.

LOBELIA
Lobelia inflata L.

Other common names: Indian tobacco, wild tobacco, bladder pod, asthma weed, gagroot, pukeweed, vomitwort, low belia, eyebright.

Range and habitat: This poisonous weed occurs nearly everywhere throughout the United States, being most plentiful east of the Mississippi River, and thriving in dry, clayey, or siliceous soil in sunny situations along roadsides, and in old fields and pastures.

Description: The erect leafy stem of this annual herbaceous plant is from 1 to 3 feet high, from a fibrous root. It is simple and rough-hairy below, smooth above, and bears a few short branches. The entire plant contains an acrid milky juice. It belongs to the bellflower family. (Campunulaceae.)

The pale green leaves are alternate, from 1 to 2.5 inches long, gradually diminishing in size as they reach the summit of the plant, the lower leaves being borne on stalks, while the upper ones are stemless. They are thin, oblong or oval, blunt, irregularly toothed, and almost wavy, with short hairs on both surfaces. From July until frost the rather inconspicuous, very small pale blue flowers appear. These are very numerous, each one borne in the axils of the upper leaves on very short stems, all together forming a long, spike-like head. The lower lip of the flower has three lobes, the upper one two segments, and from the center of the latter the tube of the flower is cleft to the base. The seed pods are in the form of inflated capsules, nearly globular, striated (grooved or marked with parallel lines), and contain very numerous minute dark-brown seeds.

Parts used: The leaves and flowering tops are used in medicine, and there is also a good demand for the seed. The leaves and tops should be gathered after some of the pods have become inflated, should be dried in the shade, and when dry kept in covered vessels. The dried leaves and tops have a rather disagreeable, somewhat sickening odor, and the taste, though mild at first, soon becomes strongly acrid and nauseous. The seeds are extremely minute, and each capsule is said to contain from 450 to 500 seeds. Lobelia is an expectorant, acts upon the nervous system and bowels, causes vomiting, and is poisonous.

Price: The price paid for the dried leaves and tops ranges from 3 to 8 cents per pound, and that for the seed from 15 to 20 cents per pound.

TANSY
Tanacetum vulgare L.

Other common names: Bitter buttons, ginger plant, parsley fern, scented fern.

Range and habitat: Tansy was originally introduced into this country as a garden plant from Europe, where it is native. It has now escaped from cultivation and is found as a weed along waysides and fences in many places from New England to Minnesota and southward to North Carolina and Missouri.

Description: This strong-scented perennial herb belongs to the aster family (Asteraceae). The stout, erect stem is from 1.5 to 3 feet high, branching near the top, somewhat reddish, and usually smooth. The general outline of the leaf is oval, and it is divided nearly to the midrib into about seven pairs of segments, which, like the terminal one, are again divided for about two-thirds of the distance to the midvein into smaller lobes having saw-toothed margins. The entire leaf is about 6 inches in length. Tansy is in flower from July to September, and the roundish but flat-topped yellow flower heads are produced in dense terminal clusters.

Parts used: At the time of flowering the leaves and tops are collected for medicinal purposes and are dried in the usual manner. The odor of tansy is strongly aromatic and the taste bitter. In drying, tansy loses about four-fifths of its weight.

Tansy is employed in derangements of women, and has stimulant and tonic properties. It is also used for expelling worms. This drug is poisonous and has been known to produce fatal results.

Imports and prices: About 30,000 pounds of tanacetum or tansy are imported annually. The price paid per pound ranges from 3 to 6 cents.

GUM PLANT
Grindelia robusta Nutt.

Range: The gum plant occurs in the states west of the Rocky Mountains.

Description: The entire plant is covered with a resinous substance, which gives it a gummy, varnished appearance, whence its common name, gum plant, is derived.

This perennial of the aster family of plants has an erect habit of growth, and sends up a round, smooth stem about a foot and a half high, narrowly grooved and freely branching near the top, each terminating The branches the flower heads have a slightly reddish appearance. The pale-green leaves are about an inch long, of a leathery texture, rather rigid, coated with resin, and show numerous translucent dots. The leaves are oblong-spatulate (having a gradually narrowed base below the broader rounded summit) and are more or less clasping at the base, the lower ones somewhat saw-toothed.

The yellow flowers are borne singly at the ends of the branches and measure about three-quarters of an inch across. The involucre (set of small leaves immediately beneath the flower) is very resinous and consists of numerous thick, over lapping scales, the tips of which are rolled forward.

Parts used and prices: The flowering tops and leaves of this and of the scaly grindelia are collected indiscriminately, and bring from 5 to 12 cents per pound. They are used in asthma and similar affections, and externally in cases of poisoning by poison ivy.

SCALY GRINDELIA
Grindelia squarrosa (Pursh) Dunal.

Range: Scaly grindelia has a wider distribution than the gum plant, being quite common on the plains and prairies from the Saskatchewan to Minnesota, south to Texas and Mexico, and westward to California.

Description: This species is very similar to the gum plant, with the exception that it is smaller, and does not have the gummy appearance of the former The slender, erect stems are from 1 to 2 feet high and somewhat sparingly branched near the top. The branches near the flower heads appear to be somewhat more reddish than in the species previously mentioned.

In this species, also, the leaves are not borne on stalks, but are somewhat clasping at the base, and they are longer (about 2 inches long), not rigid, thinner, and more prominently toothed. The flowers are also very similar to those of the gum plant, but are smaller, the scales narrower, and the recurved tips longer and more slender.

Parts used: The leaves and flowering tops are collected with those of the gum plant, Grindelia robusta.

BONESET
Eupatorium perfoliatum L.

Other common names: Thoroughwort, crosswort, wood boneset, teasel, ague-weed, feverwort, thorough-stem or thorough-wax, vegetable antimony, sweating plant, Indian sage, wild sage, tearal, wild Isaac.

Range and habitat: Boneset delights in moist situations, and is common as a weed in clayey or sandy soil, in low, wet ground, and along streams, on the edges of swamps and in thickets from the New England States west to Nebraska and south to Texas and Florida.

WEEDS USED IN MEDICINE

Description: One of the features which will aid in recognizing this plant is the peculiar arrangement of the leaves. These are opposite each other and joined together at the base around the stem, and therefore have the appearance of a single leaf with the stem passing through the center of it. Boneset is a perennial herb of the aster family of plants (Asteraceae), with stout, rough, hairy stems 1 to 5 feet high, from a horizontal, crooked root. The leaves are opposite, united at the base, lance shaped, tapering to a point, bluntly toothed, rough with prominent veins, wrinkled, dark green on the upper surface, downy and paler green on the lower surface. Both leaves together measure from 8 to 14 inches from point to point and 1 to 1.5 inches wide. The flowers are white, tubular, ten to twenty or more united in dense heads, and the heads are borne in rather crowded flat-topped clusters, appearing from July to September.

Parts used: The leaves and flowering tops are the parts used in medicine, and these should be collected when the plants are in flower, stripped from the stalk, and carefully dried. They lose about three fourths of their weight in drying. The odor is faintly aromatic, the taste bitter and astringent. As indicated by the common names "ague-weed" and "feverwort," this is a popular remedy in fever and ague. It is used also in colds, dyspepsia, jaundice, and for toning up the system. In large doses it is an emetic and cathartic.

Prices: Eupatorium or boneset leaves and tops bring from 2 to 8 cents per pound.

CATNIP
Nepeta cataria L.

Other common names: Catmint, catrup, cat's wort, field mint.

Range and habitat: This very common weed is naturalized from Europe, and is found in rather dry soil in waste places and cultivated land, about old buildings and along fences, from Canada to Minnesota and southward to Virginia and Arkansas.

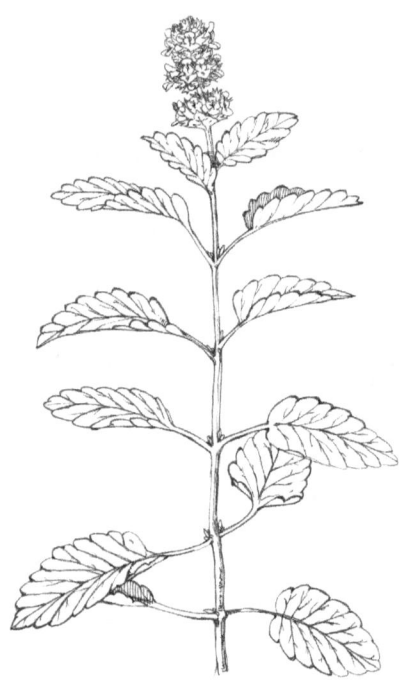

WEEDS USED IN MEDICINE

Description: The erect, square stems of this perennial herb of the mint family (Menthaceae) grow to a height of 2 to 3 feet, are branched, and somewhat whitish in appearance from the covering of fine white hairs.

The leaves are opposite and borne on stems, heart shaped or oblong, with an acute apex, 1 to 2 inches long, evenly and finely scalloped, green above, beneath grayish-green with fine white hairs. The many-flowered clusters appear from June to September, and are borne in thick spikes 1 to 5 inches long at the top of the stems and branches. The flowers are white or somewhat purple, two-lipped, the upper lip two-cleft, the lower one three-lobed and sometimes spotted with red, the middle lobe broadest and round-toothed.

Parts used: The flowering tops and leaves are to be collected when the plant is in flower and carefully dried. They have a strong mint-like odor and a bitter taste. The coarser stems and branches should be rejected. Catnip is used in derangements of women, as a mild stimulant and tonic, and has a quieting effect on the nervous system.

Imports and prices: Cataria or catnip is imported in but small quantities. The price paid for the flowering tops and leaves is from 1 to 8 cents per pound.

HOARHOUND
Marrubium vulgare L.

Other common names: Houndsbane, marvel, marube.

Range and habitat: Hoarhound has been naturalized from Europe, and has escaped from gardens in this country, being found now rather abundantly in dry sandy or stony soil in waste places, pastures, fields, along roadsides, and near dwellings, from Maine to South Carolina, Texas, and westward to California and Oregon. It is very abundant in pastures in California, Oregon, and in limited areas in Indiana, Missouri, Ohio, and Michigan. In southern California this plant has proved a most troublesome weed, occurring almost everywhere and growing in such dense masses as to crowd out all other vegetation. It has spread rapidly over thousands of acres, taking complete possession of the land and destroying pastures.

Description: The entire plant has a whitish, woolly appearance, caused by the dense covering of hairs. It is a perennial plant, and as will be seen from the characteristic lip-shaped flowers, is a member of the mint family (Menthaceae). The whole plant has a rather pleasant, balsamic odor. Hoarhound is a bushy, branching herb, with fibrous roots sending up numerous woolly stems about 1 to 3 feet high, rounded below and four-angled above. The wrinkled narrowed or somewhat heart shaped at the base, with rounded teeth, somewhat hairy and wrinkled on the upper surface, and prominently veined and very hoary on the lower surface. The flowers are whitish, two-lipped, the upper lip two-lobed, the lower three-lobed, and are borne in dense, woolly clusters in the axils of the leaves.

The plant flowers from June to September, and the characteristic hooked calyx teeth of the mature flower clusters cling to the wool of sheep like a bur, resulting in the scattering of the seeds.

Parts used: The leaves and tops are used in medicine. These should be gathered just before the herb is in flower, rejecting the coarse stalks, and should be dried in the shade in the usual manner. The balsamic odor diminishes in drying. The herb has a bitter, persistent taste. Hoarhound is well known as a remedy for colds, and is also used in dyspepsia and for expelling worms.

Imports and prices: A considerable quantity of marrubium or hoarhound is imported, about 125,000 pounds coming into this country annually. Three to eight cents is the price paid per pound.

WEEDS USED IN MEDICINE

BLESSED THISTLE
Cnicus benedictus L.

Other common names: Holy thistle, bitter thistle Our Lady's thistle, St. Benedict's thistle, cursed thistle, spotted thistle.

Range and habitat: This weed has been introduced from Europe and occurs in stony, uncultivated localities and waste places in the Southern States and in California and Utah.

Description: Blessed thistle is an annual plant belonging

to the aster family (Asteraceae). The round stems are erect, about 1 to 2 feet high, branched, and rather woolly. The leaves are more or less hairy, the lower ones borne on petioles (leaf stems), the upper ones (stemless) and clasping the stem. They are oblong-lanceolate and wavy-lobed. The terminal yellow flower heads are surrounded by scales of a leathery texture, which are prolonged into long, hard, branching spines.

Parts used: The leaves and tops should be collected when the plant is in flower, about June, thoroughly and quickly dried, and kept in a vessel from which moisture, light, and air should be excluded. They have a somewhat disagreeable odor and the taste is very bitter. Blessed thistle is employed in fevers, dyspepsia, and as a tonic to restore the appetite.

Imports and prices: This plant is cultivated in Germany, from which country it is imported to a limited extent. The price per pound ranges from 8 to 10 cents.

YARROW
Achillea millefolium L.

Other common names: Milfoil, thousand leaf, thousand-leaved clover, green arrow, gordoloba, nosebleed, bloodwort, carpenter's grass, sanguinary, soldiers' woundwort, old man's pepper.

Range and habitat: This herb is a common weed from the New England States to Missouri and in scattered localities in other parts of the country, occurring along roadsides, in old fields, pastures, and meadows.

Description: Yarrow is a perennial belonging to the aster family (Asteracese). It is about 10 to 20 inches in height, its numerous dark -green feathery leaves divided into very fine crowded parts. The flowers are produced in abundance from June to September. These are small, white (sometimes rose-colored), and are crowded in dense flat-topped heads.

The odor of yarrow is strong and aromatic, very similar to that of chamomile, and the taste is sharp and bitter. When this plant is eaten by cows its bitter taste and strong odor are imparted to dairy products.

Parts used: The entire plant is collected when in flower, and is carefully dried. The coarser stems should be rejected. The plant loses nearly four-fifths of its weight in drying. Yarrow is a stimulant tonic, acts upon the bladder, and checks excessive discharges.

Imports and prices: This is an imported article, though not brought into the United States in large quantities. The price of achillea or yarrow ranges from 2 to 5 cents per pound.

CANADA FLEABANE
Leptilon canadense (L.) Britton. (Erigeron canadensis L.)

Other common names: Horseweed, colt's tail, scabious, prideweed, butter weed, fireweed, blood-stanch, cow's tail, bitter weed.

Range and habitat: This weed is common in damp, sandy soils in fields and waste places and along roadsides in many parts of the United States, especially throughout the northern Mississippi Valley.

Description: Canada fleabane is an annual weed belonging to the aster family (Asteraceae). The stem, which is bristly-hairy, or sometimes smooth, varies greatly in height, according to the soil, being sometimes only 3 inches high, and in favorable soil often reaching a height of 10 feet. The larger plants are branched near the top. The leaves are usually somewhat hairy, those scattered along the stem being rather narrow, with unbroken margins, and the lower ones slightly toothed. From June to November numerous heads of small inconspicuous white flowers are produced, followed by an abundance of seed.

Parts used: The entire herb is medicinal, and should be gathered during the flowering period and carefully dried. It has a faint, agreeable odor and a somewhat astringent and bitter taste.

The fresh herb on distillation yields a volatile oil which is sold as oil of fleabane. The common name "blood stanch" indicates the use of this plant for arresting hemorrhages from various sources and the bleeding of wounds. It is useful also in diarrhea and dropsy.

Price: The price paid for erigeron or fleabane ranges from 6 to 8 cents per pound.

JIMSON WEED
Datura stramonium L.

Other common names: Jamestown weed (from which "jimson" weed is derived), thornapple, stinkweed, stinkwort, devil's apple, mad-apple, devil's trumpet, fireweed, Jamestown lily, dewtry, apple of Peru.

Range and habitat: Jimson weed is exceedingly common in fields and waste places throughout the entire country with the exception of the North and West. It is native in the Tropics and widely scattered in nearly all warm countries.

Description: This well-known rank and ill-scented poisonous weed is an annual about 2 to 5 feet in height, and belongs to the potato family (Solanaceae), Its yellowish- green stems are stout, leafy, and much forked. The leaves are large, 3 to 8 inches long, thin, smooth, pointed at the apex and usually narrowed at the base, irregularly waved and toothed, veiny, dark green on the upper surface and paler green beneath. The rather large, showy flowers are produced from May to September. They are white, funnel shaped, about 3 inches long, and have a heavy odor. The seed pod is a dry, oval, prickly capsule, which, when quite ripe, bursts open and discloses four valves, containing numerous black, kidney-shaped seeds. (Fig. 27.) The seeds are ill-smelling when fresh, as is the entire plant.

They are dull black, about one-sixth of an inch long, flattened, wrinkled, and marked with small depressions.

Parts used: Both the leaves and seeds are medicinal. The leaves are collected at the time of flowering, the entire plant being cut or pulled up and the leaves stripped and dried in the shade. The unpleasant narcotic odor diminishes upon drying. The leaves are poisonous, cause dilation of the pupil of the eye, and are used principally in asthma.

For the collection of the seeds the capsules should be taken from the plants when they are quite ripe, but still of a green color. The capsules should then be dried for a few days, when they will burst open and the seeds can be readily shaken out. These should now be carefully dried. The seeds like the leaves are poisonous and possess the same properties. Occasional cases of poisoning of children occur from eating the seeds of jimson weed and taking the flowers in their mouths.

WEEDS USED IN MEDICINE

Imports and prices: From 100,000 to 150,000 pounds of stramonium leaves (the name by which they are designated in the drug trade) are imported into this country annually, and about 10,000 pounds of seeds are imported. The leaves will bring from 2.5 to 8 cents per pound, and stramonium seeds from 3 to 7 cents per pound.

Purple Thorn Apple

The purple thorn-apple, technically known as Datura tatula, is very similar to the jimson weed, possesses the same properties, and is distinguished from it merely by its reddish stems and purplish flowers. The leaves and seeds may be gathered with those of the jimson weed.

POISON HEMLOCK
Conium maculatum L.

Other common names: Spotted parsley, St. Rennet's herb, bad-man's oatmeal, heck-how, wode whistle, cashes, bunk, poison parsley, spotted cowbane.

Range and habitat: Poison hemlock is rather common in waste places and along roadsides, principally in the Eastern and Middle States. It has been naturalized in this country from Europe.

Description: From the close resemblance of the leaves of this plant to parsley, it is sometimes mistaken for the latter and fatal cases of poisoning have occurred. All parts of the plant are exceedingly poisonous. Poison hemlock belongs to the same family as the parsley, namely, the Apiaceae. It is a biennial, about 2 to 6 feet in height, with a smooth, hollow stem dotted with purple, and large leaves very much like those of parsley. The numerous small white flowers are borne in rather showy umbels (flat-topped clusters, with stems from one point) and appear in June and July. The fruit ripens in August and September. The fruit is grayish-green, ribbed, about one-eighth of an inch long, ovate, laterally flattened, and smooth.

The entire plant possesses a disagreeable mousy odor, which is especially noticeable when bruised.

Parts used: The fruit and leaves are the parts used. The fruit should be collected while still green but full grown, which in most localities is some time in August. It should be dried in dark but well ventilated places, and then stored in tight cans or boxes where it will not be exposed to the action of light and air. The poison hemlock leaves should be collected when the plant is in flower, which will be in the second year of its growth. The stems should be rejected. Contrary to the usual method of drying leaves and herbs, the poison hemlock leaves may be quickly dried in the sun and then kept in tightly closed vessels. The leaves will retain their green color if properly cured. The odor is still very disagreeable, but not so pronounced as in the fresh plant.

This very poisonous drug is used in rheumatism, neuralgia, asthma, and in cases where the nervous system is in an excited condition.

Imports and prices: The imports of conium or poison hemlock seed amount to about 20,000 pounds annually, and from 10,000 to 20,000 pounds of the leaves are imported. The price paid for the seed is about 3 cents per pound, and for the leaves about 4 cents.

AMERICAN WORMSEED
Chenopodium ambrosioides L.

Other commmon names: Mexican tea, Spanish tea, Jerusalem tea, Jesuit tea, ambrosia.

Range and habitat: This strong scented herb, naturalized in this country from tropical America, frequents waste places around dwellings and is found in streets, meadows, pastures, and grain fields from New England to Florida, and westward to California.

Description: American wormseed is an annual plant of

the goosefoot family (Chenopodiaceae), attaining a height of from 2 to 3 feet. The stem is grooved, usually much branched and leafy, the leaves oblong or oblong- lance-shaped, somewhat acute at the apex, the lower ones 1 to 3 inches long and wavy-toothed, the numerous upper leaves much smaller and usually entire. From July to September the flowers are produced, followed throughout the autumn by the fruits, both of which are green and borne in crowded leafy spikes. The whole plant has a powerful, disagreeable odor, due to the essential oil which it contains.

Part used: The entire leafy part of the plant is sometimes

employed for the distillation of the oil, although the fruit alone is listed in the Pharmacopoeia of the United States. The fruit is distilled for the oil, which it contains in large quantities.

The fruits are in the form of small grains, about the size of a pin head, globular but slightly flattened, greenish, and enclosing the small shining black seeds. They have the same powerful odor as the plant, which does not diminish when the fruit is dried, and the taste is bitter and pungent. American wormseed is an anthelmintic, that is, it has the property of expelling worms. The fruits of Chenopodium anthelminticum, another species of wormseed, are collected with those of the species just described. This plant is very similar to the American wormseed, the fruits being alike, and the only differences being that in Chenopodium anthelminticum the stem is slightly taller, from 2.5 to 3.5 feet high, the leaves are more coarsely toothed, the flowers are borne in more elongated, usually leafless spikes, the odor is more pronounced and disagreeable, and the range and distribution of the plant are more limited.

Wormseed is cultivated to a considerable extent in parts of Maryland, where the distillation of the plant for the oil is carried on.

Price: In ordinary seasons the price paid for Chenopodium or wormseed ranges from 6 to 8 cents per pound. The oil distilled from wormseed is at present selling at $1.50 per pound.

BLACK MUSTARD
Brassica nigra (L.) Koch. (Sinapis nigra L.)

Other common names: Brown mustard, red mustard.

Range and habitat: Black mustard, introduced from Europe, is a troublesome weed in many parts of the United States. It is common in almost every State in the Union along roadsides, in cultivated ground, and in waste places, being especially troublesome in grain fields and pastures. Both black and white mustards are cultivated in California.

This plant is a great pest in southern California, covering thousands of acres and forming dense, impenetrable thickets over 6 feet in height, in which birds have their nesting places, and, by eating and excreting the seeds, help to spread this pernicious weed.

Description: The rather stiff, dark-green, branching stem of black mustard is from 4 to 6 feet in height. The lower part of the stem and branches is more or less bristly hairy, but the upper part is usually smooth. The leaves are dark green, somewhat rough, with bristly hairs, and are all borne on stalks. The lower leaves are lobed, the terminal lobe being the largest and the two or more lateral ones smaller. The leaves toward the top of the plant become lance shaped and are slightly toothed.

The flowers of black mustard appear from June to September, and are of a bright yellow color. They are rather small, scarcely a quarter of an inch in diameter, the four petals spreading and each consisting of a rounded blade with a narrow claw. The petals alternate with the pale-green sepals or calyx lobes. The flowers appear in clusters at the ends of the elongating stems, followed from July to November by the numerous erect pods crowded against the stem in dense narrow clusters. The pods are about 1 inch in length, quadrangular, smooth, and tipped at the apex by the short, persistent style. The seeds contained in the pods are very numerous, small, about one twenty-fifth of an inch in diameter, globular, blackish brown, and finely pitted.

The plant is an annual, and if care is taken to prevent the distribution of the seeds it is not difficult to exterminate. The seeds possess great vitality, and may remain in the ground for years before germinating.

Collection of seeds: The tops may be pulled when most of the pods are nearly mature, but before they are ready to spring open. They should then be placed on a clean, dry floor or shelf, allowing the pods to ripen and dry out, when they will burst open and the seeds can be readily shaken out. Mustard seed has no odor whatever when collected, not even when it is powdered in its dry state, but as soon as water is added in grinding it, the powerful, penetrating mustard odor is developed. The taste is sharp and pungent.

WHITE MUSTARD
Sinapis alba L.

Another common name: Yellow mustard.

Range and habitat: White mustard is a weed found in cultivated land along waysides and fence rows, but is not so abundant nor so widely distributed as the black mustard. It is naturalized in this country from Europe.

Description: This plant is very similar to black mustard, but is smaller (growing only about 1 to 2 feet tall), bright green, but the flowers and seeds are much larger, and the rough-hairy pods with their long, sickle-shaped beaks are spreading instead of being pressed against the stem. The flowers are paler yellow than those of the foregoing species. The divisions of the leaves reach to the midrib, the leaves are rough-hairy, and the pods bristly. The seeds are pale yellow and smooth.

Collection and uses of seeds: The seeds are to be collected in the same manner as those of black mustard. White mustard seed has no odor in its entire state, and when water is added in grinding it the odor does not become so pronounced as in the case of black mustard, neither is the taste so pungent.

In medicine mustard seeds are used principally in the preparation of plasters and poultices. They are used also in dyspepsia, and in large doses act as an emetic.

Imports and prices: The imports into the United States of black and white mustard together during the fiscal year ended June 30, 1903, amounted to 5,302,876 pounds. The price ranges from 3 to 6 cents both the black and white mustard seeds.

THE END